JESUS
//THE DEFINITION OF GOD

Seeing the Love of the Father through the Life of the Son

WRITTEN BY:
DEAN SHROPSHIRE

Jesus—The Definition of God
ISBN: 978-1-936314-63-8

P.O. Box 22
Hobbs, New Mexico 88240

Published by Word and Spirit Publishing
P.O. Box 701403
Tulsa, Oklahoma 74170

TABLE OF CONTENTS

PREFACE

John 8:31-32 says, "Then said Jesus to those Jews which believed on him (and you too, if you believe), If ye continue in my word, then are ye my disciples indeed; And ye shall know the truth, and the truth shall make you free" (explanation mine). What a promise! What an opportunity for those of you in God's family to know not only His Word but to be filled with His very presence and capable of knowing His perfect will for your life as demonstrated by Jesus! Jesus went on to say in John 8:36, "If the Son therefore shall make you free, ye shall be free indeed." You need to pay attention to what you're reading. Too many are not experiencing (let alone enjoying) what Jesus paid for on the cross! It's time to embrace the truth and experience the freedom that belongs to you in Jesus Christ.

There is no way I could share all that is on my heart concerning the finished work of Jesus in just one book, but the character and operation of God will only be understood by those who see Jesus as He truly is. My prayer is that when you are finished reading this book, you will never stop seeking the freedom He paid for in every area of your life! There's a chance your theological toes may be stepped on, but I encourage you to continue reading and receive what the Spirit of God has to say.

Open your heart. God's Word (as you know) is Spirit. John 6:63 says, "It is the spirit that quickeneth; the flesh profiteth nothing: the words that I speak unto you, they are spirit, and they are life."

God's Word is aimed at your spirit (heart), not your mind. Your mind will become renewed in the process but it all begins when you approach the Word as a little child. In Luke 18:17, Jesus said, "Verily I say unto you, Whosoever shall not receive the kingdom of God as a little child shall in no wise enter therein." Get ready! There's more to learn and Jesus authored every bit of it.

Pastor Dean

//Chapter One

SOMETHING'S WRONG

I came to a point in my life many years ago when I realized that something was terribly wrong with my understanding of the Word of God. There were too many inconsistencies between what I was taught and what I saw taking place around me. As a young boy, I was raised in a mainstream denominational church, one that stressed the inerrancy of

God's Word. For years (more years than I care to mention), I lived a life of separation from the very One who paid for my abundant life. Even though I had received Jesus as my Lord and Savior, there was no tangible evidence of that in my life. I had never been taught or trained in God's Word effectively and consequently, I hadn't experienced what Jesus paid for on the cross.

I began to realize that something was wrong. Wrong in the sense that my life in no way reflected what I now know belonged to me through the power of God's Word! The problem wasn't the Word of God, but how it was taught and how I received it. Not to mention, those doing the teaching were not reflecting what was being taught! I know people aren't perfect but Jesus said, "You will know them by their fruit!" (Matthew 7:20.)

Proverbs 22:6 says, "Train up a child in the way he should go: and when he is old (or continues to grow), he will not depart from it" (explanation mine). I am referencing this verse because what I was taught growing up did not position me to walk as this scripture states a child should walk when properly trained. I'm not throwing rocks but simply stating that if this verse is true, along with Ephesians 6:4 in the New Testament which says, "And, ye fathers, provoke not your children to wrath (exasperation and anger): but bring them up in the nurture (training to include discipline in spirit, soul and body) and admonition of the Lord" (explanation mine), then you realize too that something's wrong with the way the Word is being taught, not just to children, but to people sitting in church services across the country today.

There are more people falling off the bandwagon than jumping on it seems! Why is that? Because people are not being exposed to *real truth* in regard to the goodness of God. Maybe you have experienced what I did as a youth and have not yet come to understand how much God loves you. Like me, you might not have been exposed to the *real truth* and are still struggling in life. Please don't be discouraged, just continue reading. There is *real* hope and God will see to it that you experience all He has for you if you will only believe. God loves you and before you've finished this book, you'll know that for certain.

I don't mind telling you that it makes me a little angry when I reflect on the part of my life lived in the shadow of truth. Mad not just at those who didn't know or pursue the truth, but angry that I didn't jump in with both feet to find out just how big God is on my own. My prayer for you is that you will read something that will encourage or provoke you to search the Scriptures for yourself.

If you are sincere about your relationship with God, He will reveal Himself to you and direct you to others who are just as hungry. You need not be concerned about ending up around the wrong people or in the wrong place. Your Heavenly Father (as revealed through the life of Jesus) is easy to follow. His ways bring encouragement and life so even the youngest Christian can be confident in

His leading. I love what Jesus said in Luke 12:31-32, "But rather seek ye the kingdom of God (His character and way of operating); and all these things (whatever you need in this life) shall be added unto you. Fear not, little flock; for it is your Father's good pleasure to give you the kingdom" (explanation mine). Jesus revealed this to you so you would realize that God wants you in His family with all that encompasses. God wants you to have all Jesus paid for, that's why He *defined* His will through His Son.

When my wife Kathy and I made a commitment to marriage in August of 1978, we also made a commitment to reconnect with the church. We were both raised in the same denomination so we started attending where we were comfortable. I didn't hear or see much that was different from when I left the church in my late teen years. Even though it was in a different city, the church looked the same. The songs were the same, the unhappy looks on the members' faces were the same and the worst part was feeling a sense of unworthiness and hopelessness. Joy was non-existent; there was no victory and nothing reflected the goodness of God! There was something wrong!

We continued faithfully in our attendance, but one Sunday while we were getting ready for church, we turned on the television and began watching a preacher named Fred Price. I was immediately taken aback by Dr. Price's boldness and confidence concerning the Word of God. He not only believed what he was saying but also expected it to change his life. That day changed our lives forever. We continued going to our church, but each week left empty in light of what we'd heard before leaving the house. Now, don't be upset with me, I'm just trying to get you to understand that God has a lot more in store for you! As Paul tells you in Ephesians 3:20-21, "Now unto him that is able to do exceeding abundantly above all that we ask or think, according to the power that worketh in us, unto him be glory in the church by Christ Jesus throughout all the ages, world without end, Amen."

I'm not just speaking specifically about where you are presently attending church, but if you're not continuing to grow and are not producing great fruit to the glory of God then something's wrong! My intention in writing this book is to challenge and provoke you to move further than you ever thought possible. All you have to do is hunger for more. The victory is not going to come unless you believe, speak and do your part.

Why is it difficult for some to comprehend that the Heavenly Father wants everyone to enjoy life on earth as well as eternal life? Have they become so spiritually minded that they have forgotten God's will is to be relevant in this life? Jesus said in Matthew 7:11, "If ye then, being evil, know how to give good gifts unto your children, how much more shall your Father which is in heaven give good things to them that ask him?" Glory to God! It's time you realize how much God loves you and how much He wants to prosper and cause you to be a blessing just as He is! If all you have heard is that God is critical, judgmental or schizophrenic, then you've been given the WRONG information! He loves you and wants the best for you: spirit, soul and body. Through His Word and by His Spirit, you will learn to enjoy and reflect His goodness.

PRAY THIS//

Father, thank You for sending Jesus so that I could live an abundant life now and spend eternity with You, in Jesus' name, Amen.

CONFESS THIS//

I am hungry for God's Word and I am challenged to study the Word for myself to find out what He has promised me and live the abundant life Jesus provided for me every day!

//CHAPTER TWO

A HELPER

Do you realize people need help? Kathy and I needed help. I don't mean financially or naturally, but we needed spiritual help. We were still attending church and watching Fred Price, along with several other ministers who seemed to have his same fervor and demeanor, but we hadn't taken advantage of the *real Helper*!

When I first moved to Hobbs, New Mexico, before Kathy and I were married, I worked for a man and he and his wife were Spirit-filled believers. They had been involved with a non-denominational church for several years, but the denomination Kathy and I were affiliated with and had been a part of all our lives did not accept this Spirit-filled business as a part of their doctrine. As a matter of fact, we had been exposed to very adamant teaching about the Spirit's legitimacy in the church today.

My first month in Hobbs, I had to live with my boss and his wife until an apartment became available. That is when the fun began. We were working fairly long days so when we got home, we didn't do much before we called it a day. I was sleeping on the living room couch every night. My boss would go to bed and his wife would come into the living room, sit across from me on the coffee table and would proceed to instruct me concerning this *Helper*, who is the Holy Spirit. She would assure me how much I needed this *Helper* in life to guide me in my future as well as my marriage. I was pinned down, so to speak, and I couldn't get away! I was a captive audience and not always receptive, I might add. (Hey, she was my boss' wife and I could only do so much!) Occasionally, my boss would come in the living room to try and encourage her to quit bugging me, but you know how much weight men carry when it comes to their wives sharing their faith!

On weekends, when I went to El Paso to see Kathy, I would fill her and my parents in on the information that my boss' wife shared with me. We thought they were off theologically because we all had the same church background. My dad went a step further and encouraged me to stay away from this misguided couple.

Well, Kathy and I didn't stay away. Before too long, we accepted the invitation for them to pray with us to receive the infilling of the Holy Spirit! One night, in one moment, we were both filled with the Holy Spirit and spoke with other tongues and our lives were changed forever!

Mark 16:17 says, "And these signs shall follow them that believe; In my name shall they cast out devils; they shall speak with new tongues" and Acts 2:4 says, "And they were all filled with the Holy Ghost, and began to speak with other tongues, as the Spirit gave them utterance."

Thank God for this couple and their passion for people! Because of their obedience, Kathy and I were able to access all Jesus paid for us to receive when He died on the cross. I wanted to make mention of them because I don't believe most Spirit-filled Christians understand how important it is to share this life changing experience with those who are receptive. Their willingness to share this gift changed our lives, our girls' lives and the lives of thousands who've exposed themselves to our church and ministry.

The Holy Spirit's presence in your life, as outlined in the Word of God, is vital in order for you to have success in your walk with your Heavenly Father. Jesus told His disciples before He left the earth that He was going to send them another Comforter, Helper, Teacher, Strengthener, Truth Bearer. Yes, He was speaking of the Holy Spirit, the third member of the Godhead. Notice these words of Jesus found in John 15:26, "But when the Comforter is come, whom I will send unto you from the Father, even the Spirit of Truth, which proceedeth from the Father, he shall testify of me." And then in John 16:13 Jesus said, "Howbeit when he, the Spirit of Truth, is come, he will guide you into all truth: for he shall not speak of himself; but whatsoever he shall hear, that shall he speak: and he will shew you things to come." The phrase, "he shall not speak of himself" is very interesting in light of Jesus being the **definition** of God. This one statement reveals the operation of the Holy Spirit, as well as Jesus, as being the reflection and revelation of God, of His character and perfect will for mankind.

Kathy and I began to realize that this Gospel was indeed good news and totally relevant to our lives.

We immediately started seeing God's Word as *His* Word and as we applied it to our lives, we began to experience results we never thought possible. After we received the Holy Spirit (as Jesus described in Acts 1:4-5, "And, being assembled together with them, commanded them that they should not depart from Jerusalem, but wait for the promise of the Father, which, saith he, ye have heard of me. For John truly baptized with water; but ye shall be baptized with the Holy Ghost not many days hence."), the simplicity of God's plan became more and more evident. What once seemed to be an endless list of do's and don'ts, maybe and maybe not's, changed into everyday principles we could receive, apply and enjoy based on this new righteous relationship God had entered into with us through Jesus. It was no longer about us; it was about the Greater One, Jesus, and what He had provided for us through His death, burial and resurrection. It was no longer about what we could do to attain this life, but how childlike faith would cause us great gain.

PRAY THIS//

Father, thank You for sending the Holy Spirit to help, advocate, teach, coach and intercede on my behalf. I will yield myself to His leading daily because He is the revealer of all truth, in Jesus' name, Amen.

CONFESS THIS//

I am filled with the Holy Spirit by faith and I speak with other tongues as the Spirit gives me utterance.

//Chapter Three

TRADITION OR TRUTH

Do you have any idea how deceived the Church has been because of the traditions of men? I'm not talking about true Biblical traditions, but rather the traditions men have perpetrated on the Church because of their personal misguided agendas! I didn't say they weren't well meaning and sincere. I'm simply pointing out their unwillingness to see that Jesus is the express image and **definition** of God. People have been exposed to so many lies concerning Jesus and the Gospel that it's no wonder they are confused about the character of God.

I believe the reason most people stay in the dark is because they are unwilling to embrace the Holy Spirit as the Revelator of Scripture. He is the one who not only fills you, but also creates in you the desire and hunger for more than just a religious experience. John said of Jesus in Matthew 3:11, "I indeed baptize you with water unto repentance. But he that cometh after me is mightier than I, whose shoes I am not worthy to bear: he shall baptize you with the Holy Ghost, and with fire." This baptism with the Holy Spirit and fire makes a drastic difference in your ability to understand and walk in the promises and power of God! The Word of God is not about traditions, but about truth that will actually set you free.

When I'm talking about Jesus being the express image or **definition** of God, I am referencing

Hebrews 1:1-3 "God, who at sundry times (many times) and in divers manners (many ways) spake in time past unto the fathers by the prophets, hath in these last days spoken unto us by His Son, whom he hath appointed heir of all things, by whom also he made the worlds; Who being the brightness (reflection) of his glory (opinion, judgment and promised condition), and the express image of his person, (precise reproduction in every respect) and upholding all things by the word of his power, when he had by himself purged our sins, sat down on the right hand of the majesty on high" (explanations mine). If Jesus was the express image or **definition** of God, as you've just read, then you must realize that everything He did or didn't do was the perfect picture of God's will.

I have always felt that the church hasn't placed enough focus on what Jesus said and did as He walked the earth. You must understand who Jesus was when He walked the earth—He was God in the flesh. What does Hebrews 1:2 say? "Hath in these last days (the days you are now living in) spoken unto us by his Son" (explanation mine). Jesus was what? He was the express image or **definition** of God! Take a moment to think about that some more before you continue reading. By virtue of Jesus being the "express image" or **definition** of God, and the "brightness of his glory," you can see that His actions and communication supersede all the types, shadows and examples given before or after His ministry.

In John 14:9, Jesus told Philip, "He that hath seen me hath seen the Father." No other person—past, present or future—can make that claim but Jesus, the Son and express image of God. Why then would anyone determine the character of God and His will for humanity by any other standard? His will was exemplified through the life of Jesus. Acts 10:38 says, "How God anointed Jesus of Nazareth with the Holy Ghost and with power: who went about doing good, and healing all that were oppressed of the devil; for God was with him."

Unless you see God for who He really is and know His heart, then even as His child, you'll fall far short of enjoying the promises He's provided. The negative, condemning, judgmental picture of God that most people have been exposed to is a perversion of God's Word and hinders the advancement of the Gospel and its intended results. I know Jesus is building His Church, but can you imagine how much quicker that will happen if the members of His body are headed in the same direction, believing and speaking the same things? When you, as God's child, begin to see Him as something more than some cosmic bully arbitrarily weaving some mysterious plan, things will be much clearer to you and you'll be able to communicate truth to the lost world you've been commissioned to tell of His goodness.

One of the great ministries of the Holy Spirit is to bring God's people into one mind and one accord. God does not author confusion in the church, and the Holy Spirit is perfectly capable of bringing order and wisdom to those who truly receive His ministry. Tradition has portrayed the church as a confused entity or organization. Even though they are reading the same book, churches seem to have very little in common. Remember, Jesus said, "He that hath seen me hath seen the Father." If that truly is the case, then maybe some who say they believe in God have missed the **definition** of God, JESUS!

My goal is not to offend or demean you, but simply inspire you to pursue a greater understanding of God's will and purpose for your life. God doesn't want some God/servant relationship with you, but desires that you have an intimate understanding of His devotion and love for you, which you see in the life of Jesus. Jesus demonstrated the relationship with the Heavenly Father as it was supposed to be: always motivated by love and trust with no fear or worry at any time. Don't continue with negative, religious mindsets that have trapped so many of God's children. Allow

His goodness and patience to bring you to a place of understanding where enjoyment and pleasure become yours now! These promises are not just for the hereafter.

Take a look at Mark 7:13 where Jesus was approached by the scribes and Pharisees concerning His disciples and their eating habits. In verse 13, Jesus rebukes the scribes and Pharisees for what they have done, saying, "Making the word of God of none effect through your tradition, which ye have delivered: and many such things do ye." The same holds true today when it comes to the traditions of men and how they've compromised the power and purpose of God that was reflected through Jesus.

I don't care what men have to say. Jesus said in John 12:32 "And I, if I be lifted up from the earth, (not the plans and ideas of man) I will draw all men unto me" (explanation mine). You don't need to promote your agenda or perception.

Simply lift up the perfect image and **definition** of God—Jesus—and watch the Church grow.

Pray This//

Father, thank You for showing me Your desire for me to have an intimate understanding of Your devotion and love as I read Your Word, in Jesus' name, Amen.

Confess This//

I know that Jesus walked this earth as God in the flesh. He did only what He saw the Father do and it was always good. God is good and He has great things in store for me.

//Chapter Four

I AND THE FATHER

I would like to discuss further the relationship that Jesus had with the Father God. Many times the Word is skimmed over in reading or tuned out when it comes to their relationship. The diligence you give to your hearing as well as your reading goes a long way in allowing the Holy Spirit to reveal truth to you and not just a mental concept.

Many people have a mental concept of God and the Lord Jesus, but you must KNOW THEM in order to understand Their character and will for humanity. What happens when you read or hear the Word spoken as if it were just an old book with words on a page? You will surely miss how valuable it can be! Proverbs 4:20-22 says, "My son, attend (pay attention) to my words; incline (stretch or bend) thine ear unto my sayings. Let them not depart from thine eyes; keep them in the midst of thine heart. For they are life unto those that find them, and health (remedy, cure or medicine) to all their flesh" (explanation mine). The Word of God, unlike any other book, must be correctly or rightly divided in order to enjoy the modern day benefits intended for every believer. Because it's divided into Old and New Testaments, you must be able to see how each part applies to you in light of your own personal relationship with Jesus and the Father. Again, if you don't see God's Word as being relevant for this present day, then why waste the time to hear or read it?

In 2 Timothy 2:15, you see how important it is to understand how to approach and apply the Word of God. It says, "Study to shew thyself approved unto God, a workman that needeth not to be ashamed, rightly dividing the word of truth." It's obvious that if the Word can be *rightly divided,* it can also be *wrongly divided.* I submit to you that most of the body of Christ haven't fully appreciated what belongs to them because they have not personally *rightly divided* the Word as it applies to their lives. Since Paul wrote approximately two-thirds of the New Testament, I believe you can put credence in the revelation he presents. However, you have access to more information than Paul did, which should cause you to be better informed and better equipped than any person who has gone before you. You have the entire Word of God to draw from, the Holy Spirit of truth to assist you, and the promise in Matthew 7:7 that if you seek you will find. There is absolutely no reason for you, as a born again believer, to walk in darkness in any area of your life when God has given you the light of His Word to illuminate your path.

One other reference I'd like to look at is 2 Timothy 3:16-17, "All scripture is given by inspiration of God, and is profitable for doctrine, for reproof, for correction, for instruction in righteousness: That the man of God may be perfect, thoroughly furnished unto all good works." Here you see what God's Word is intended to do for all who have become righteous by virtue of simply accepting Jesus. This righteousness you have now has given you access to a relationship with God, in order for your life to demonstrate His goodness just as Jesus did. Sounds like big shoes to fill but the key is, Jesus is standing in them with you. If Jesus spoke it or did it, you can count on the fact that it was the perfect will of God and an exact reflection of God's will. These verses you just read show the value of the Word of God and also its intent to help you grow in the understanding that you are made righteous in Christ Jesus. You have authority and power because of your right standing with the Heavenly Father.

Let's look at some real meat concerning Jesus being the **definition** of God. In John 10:30, Jesus said, "I and my Father are one." What does that mean to you? Do you understand the significance of Jesus and the Father being one? Would that lead you to believe that they were inseparable in their thoughts and actions? Jesus knew His position with the Father. He wasn't being presumptuous or arrogant; He simply knew who He was. Jesus saw Himself equal with and a reflection of God's perfect will for mankind during His earthly ministry. Now, that may seem like a wild statement, especially in light of how Paul described Jesus in Philippians 2:6. However, Paul was endeavoring to train believers, especially Gentiles who were foreign to the reality of an eternal God and who had spent their lives pleasing themselves through fleshly satisfaction and idol worship. He was endeavoring to teach them that their lives as believers should now be spent on "perfectly pleasing the Father" just as Jesus did, in everything they said and did. In our natural families today, the statement would never be made that a son is equal to his father, but our God is triune, so much bigger than even the parallel we can wrap our natural minds around. The Father, the Son, and the Holy Spirit are ONE, but yet they are three. Religion and traditions of men have done as much as possible to create confusion about the character of the Father and the life of the Son. If you tolerate those in your life, you will have trouble walking by faith and receiving the great love of our precious Father. If you will reduce this verse to literal truth and actually see its "right now" relevance, it will change almost everything you believe concerning God's will for your life. When you see this verse in this light, you will see what Jesus did, as well as what He didn't do, as the perfect will of God for you. What He did for others, what He said to others, how He treated others is the perfect reflection of God and the blueprint for your faith.

Let me back this up with further proof of the oneness of Father and Son. John 1:1-5, 14 says, "In the beginning was the Word, and the Word was with God, and the Word was God. The same was in the beginning with God. All things were made by him; and without him was not anything made that was made. In him was life; and the life was the light of men. And the light shineth in darkness; and the darkness comprehended it not. And the Word was made flesh, and dwelt among us, (and we beheld his glory, the glory as of the only begotten of the Father), full of grace and truth." These verses clearly reflect the oneness of Jesus and the Father God and you see that all Jesus said and did was the perfect will of the Father. If it was God's will then, it's His will now. Another verse of confirmation is Mark 1:11, "And there came a voice from heaven, saying, Thou art my beloved Son, in whom I am well pleased." Of course this was God speaking and He was acknowledging Jesus as His Son and would continue to speak, direct and perform through

Him all that was necessary for mankind to see His goodness.

God and Jesus are one. They work in unison and as a child of God today you should take on that same assignment. Whatever God wanted done, He could count on Jesus doing it without question or concern. This picture should become increasingly clearer to all of you who have ears to hear.

At one point, the Jews were angry at Jesus for healing on the Sabbath and He responded in John 5:19-20 by saying, "Then answered Jesus and said unto them, Verily, Verily, I say unto you, The Son can do nothing of himself, but what he seeth the Father do; for what things so ever he doeth, these also doeth the Son likewise. For the Father loveth the Son, and sheweth him all things that himself doeth; and he will shew him greater works than these, that ye may marvel." Whatever Jesus saw, He did. Whatever Jesus heard, He did. Whatever God wanted done, that is exactly what Jesus did 100% of the time. If Jesus did it then you automatically know that God was behind it. If Jesus heard God say it, then He made it audible for those who had ears to hear. If Jesus saw God do it, then He made it visible to those who had eyes to see. Do you have ears to hear and eyes that see? If so, it should be easy for you from this point forward to take your faith to another level. Jesus did the perfect will of God all the time for all people who would simply believe. Your faith in what Jesus did and your realizing it was the perfect will of God will set you up for more in every area of your life, period.

Let's take it a step further and look at John 14:10, "Believest thou not that I am in the Father, and the Father is in me? The words that I speak unto you I speak not of myself; but the Father that dwelleth in me, he doeth the works." If it took place through the ministry of Jesus, then it must have been the perfect will of God. If it was the perfect will of God, then do you suppose His will has changed?

This is the most daunting question in the body of Christ today. What is the will of God? You have access to the answer when you begin to look at and believe what Jesus did. All too often, you hear about bad things that are supposedly the will of God. Jesus **defined** the perfect will of God and any who suppose differently or teach differently are in error or deception. Did Jesus ever make anyone sick? Of course not, so why do you hear people say that God will sometimes make you sick to teach you a lesson, get your attention or worse yet, punish you for some sin you've committed? If you don't know the answer to these situations, you better get with it because your health and life depend on what you believe, not simply your genetics.

Did Jesus ever rob anyone or ever say that they would just have to suffer and do without because of their present station in life? Of course He didn't, because He's the Good Shepherd, not the stingy, mean shepherd. The names of God would not be Jehovah Rapha and Jehovah Jireh if He weren't the Healer and the Provider. His provision (spirit, soul and body) is for all His children, not just a select few in select countries.

You've heard that God wants some people blessed and some impoverished, but Jesus never taught that warped theology. His reflection of the Father was always perfect health and net-breaking abundance. Is this picture becoming clear enough for you? Really, Jesus perfectly **defined** the will of God. He said it was the Father in Him. It's just like Jesus said, "I and the Father are one." From this point forward, there is no excuse for you to become or remain traditionally bound when it comes to the will of God. Remember, if you are really seeing Jesus, then you are really seeing the Father because they are one in purpose and production. Jesus is God **defined** and when you see Him that way, He will be that way for you.

Pray This//

Father, thank You for helping me to see that the life of Jesus as He walked this earth was a perfect reflection of Your heart and will for my life today in every way, in Jesus' name, Amen.

Confess This//

Jesus did the perfect will of God all the time and the results were always life, healing and wholeness. He is a good God.

//CHAPTER FIVE

WHAT WOULD JESUS DO?

We've all heard the question, "What would Jesus do?" The question should actually be, "What did Jesus do and if He did do it, does He still want it to happen today?" Hebrews 13:8 says, "Jesus Christ the same yesterday, and today, and forever." This is the answer to the question. ALL the promises of God are for today. The Word clearly says in 2 Corinthians 1:19-20, "For the Son of God, Jesus Christ, who was preached among you by us, even by me and Silvanus and Timotheus, was not yea and nay (yes or no), but in him was yea (yes). For all (how many?) the promises of God in him (Jesus) are yea (yes), and in him Amen, unto the glory of God by us" (explanation mine).

Are you putting some of this together? If not, then re-read the scriptures and let the Spirit of God take away the doubt. John 8:32 says, "And ye shall know the truth, and the truth shall make you free." This is a benefit of continuing in the Word of God. Freedom has always been God's will for His children but the power of tradition has negated the power of God's Word in the lives of many Christians. Many faithful, church-going Christians have led lives of mediocrity because those they follow have not equated what Jesus did with the perfect will of God for mankind today.

Why should you ask what Jesus would do if you have examples in the Word of God of what He did? Why is what He did no longer what He wants to do now? Have you ever heard someone say, "Well, if it's God's will..."? What is God's will? Glad you asked! God's will is God's Word. Jesus showed you the will of the Father God. I hear you saying, "That was then," but are you forgetting that *Jesus is the same yesterday, today and forever*? The will of God hasn't changed because Jesus hasn't changed and neither has the Word. People change but God never changes.

Hebrews 10:8-10 says, "Above when he said, Sacrifice and offering and burnt offerings and offering for sin thou wouldest not, neither hadst pleasure therein; which are offered by the law; Then said he, Lo, I come to do thy will, O God. He taketh away the first, that he may establish the second. By the which will we are sanctified through the offering of the body of Jesus Christ once for all." What you see in these verses is a clear sign of Jesus coming and doing the will of God. From the beginning of His ministry to His resurrection, Jesus did the perfect will of God for all mankind, all the time. He came as the one and only perfect sacrifice for mankind; replacing the animal sacrifices and traditions that were in place before He came. You know what Jesus is doing today? The same things He was doing when He walked the earth. These things still happen in and through those who believe in who He really is and are willing themselves to trust God for the promised outcome.

The question is no longer, "What would Jesus do," but "What will you do with what Jesus paid for you to have?" In John 14:12 Jesus said, "Verily, verily, I say unto you, He that believeth on me, the works that I do shall he do also; and greater works than these shall he do; because I go unto my Father." It looks to me as if Jesus expected the things He was doing to continue, doesn't it? Again, should you accept what Jesus said at face value and allow the Father's will to continue or are you going to sit back and watch others work with Him to build the Church? Jesus did what He did to show you what you have access to and can accomplish in Him. Don't let traditionalists hold you back. Jesus is the **definition** of God and you can be the **definition** of Jesus in the life of others. The choice is yours.

PRAY THIS//

Father, I will not live in mediocrity as a believer because I see in Your Word Your perfect will for mankind today and I walk in it, in Jesus' name, Amen.

CONFESS THIS//

I will continue what Jesus started and work with Him to build the Church!

//Chapter Six

WHAT ABOUT FAITH?

It would be impossible to discuss this or any other subject in the Word of God without addressing the need for faith. Faith, which is trust and reliance on who Jesus is and what He accomplished, is the foundation for seeing Him as the **definition** of God. Hebrews 11:1 says, "Now faith is the substance of things hoped for, the evidence of things not seen." The New Living Bible says, "Faith is the confidence that what we hope for will actually happen; it gives us assurance about things we cannot yet see." The Message Bible says, "The fundamental fact of existence is that this trust in God, this faith, is the firm foundation under everything that makes life worth living. It's our handle on what we can't see." And the Amplified translation reads, "Now faith is the assurance (the confirmation, the title deed) of the things [we] hope for, being the proof of things [we] do not see and the conviction of their reality [faith perceiving as real fact what is not revealed to the senses]."

Strong's Concordance defines faith as "the conviction that God exists and is the creator and ruler of all things, the provider and bestower of eternal salvation through Christ; a strong and welcome conviction or belief that Jesus is the Messiah, through whom you obtain eternal salvation in the kingdom of God, to listen, yield to and obey God's Word."

If you truly believe in the Lord Jesus and the New Covenant you have entered into through Him, you should be able to see the will of God as an ever-present will, not something that was simply for a season. You live in the dispensation of grace or what is often called the Church Age. This simply means that the favor and grace of God is covering the earth as Jesus is building His Church.

According to these definitions of faith, you can readily see that many who have not received or even recognized the Lordship of Jesus have no way of seeing Him as the **definition** of anything. Some don't recognize the legitimacy of the New Testament and some refuse to see Jesus as the Son of God. I believe in both the legitimacy of the New Testament and that Jesus is the Son of God, so that sets me up to also see Jesus as the **definition** of God. If you also are a believer in the Lord Jesus, then perhaps you should begin to believe what He said. You have already read that Jesus always did what the Father said. At this point, begin to reprogram yourself to the truth. Don't allow tradition to continue to dictate your destiny and pursuit of the truth.

Jesus paid far too great a price for you to simply get by. You are supposed to be *overcoming* in every area of your life. Jesus said in John 10:10, "The thief cometh not, but for to steal, and to kill, and to destroy: I am come that they might have life, and that they might have it more abundantly."

Can you see how much further along you would be if you really believed Jesus did the perfect will of God and He hasn't stopped? This is the Good News you should be proclaiming. As a Christian, you have the answers for those living in darkness and bondage. First John 3:8 says, "He that committeth sin is of the devil; for the devil sinneth from the beginning. For this purpose the Son of God (the Son of who?) was manifested, that he might destroy the works of the devil" (commentary mine). That's what Jesus did, but how many are enjoying His victory? Think about how many people the enemy destroys through poverty, sickness, and bondage. Some even claim God as the author of these things. Many have allowed doubt peddlers and sight walkers to hinder their faith in God.

Consider these words from Mark 9:23, "Jesus said unto him, If thou canst believe, all things are possible to him that believeth." Do you believe this? Can you see what Jesus did for others as God's perfect will for you also? Is it possible that your doubt and unbelief is keeping you from something that has been yours since Jesus paid for it? Jesus is the **definition** of God and when you believe it, you will receive it.

PRAY THIS//

I believe Jesus is the **definition** of God and I receive all the promises in the Word by faith, in Jesus' name, Amen.

CONFESS THIS//

I see what Jesus did for others as God's perfect will for me.

//Chapter Seven

RELEVANCE NOT RELIGION

Is your religion relevant to your everyday life? Does your church experience promote and encourage you to live a victorious life? Do you understand that what Jesus did is relevant to every area of your life? Are you excited enough about what Jesus did for you to cause you to make changes in your life and live for Him? If you are unsure about the answer to any of these questions, please pay close attention. Your relationship with God and your Christian experience were designed by God to bring you to a place of victory: spirit, soul and body in this life.

Because Jesus is the **definition** of God, your life should be the **definition** of Him in the lives of others. John 15:7-8, "If ye abide in me, and my words abide in you, ye shall ask what ye will, and it shall be done unto you. Herein is my Father glorified, that ye bear much fruit; so shall ye be my disciples." Fruit (activity in your life that expresses God's will) is what brings attention to your Father God. God receives recognition today the same way He did when Jesus walked the earth—through you reflecting His perfect will.

People don't need to hear how bad they are, they need to hear and see how good God is. Religion or a form of godliness is not relevant. What makes a difference in the lives of people is rubber-meets-the-road principles that they can apply to every area of their lives. John 17:20-23 says, "Neither pray I for these alone, but for them also which shall believe on me through their word; that they all may be one; as thou, Father, art in me, and I in thee, that they also may be one in us: that the world may believe that thou hast sent me. And the glory which thou gavest me I have given them; that they may be one, even as we are one: I in them, and thou in me, that they may be made perfect in one; and that the world may know that thou hast sent me, and hast loved them, as thou hast loved me." Here's the Pastor Dean paraphrase for a portion of this passage: *You are in the family, you enjoy the benefits and everyone around you can see the love God has for you and the love He reflects through you.*

God's design has always been that your life as a believer would reflect the Jesus you received and your life would be **defined** by His will. He desires that the Greater One in you would bring definitive proof of His present day ministry, not irrelevant, ritualistic activity. Paul spoke about this in Ephesians 2:5-7, "Even when we were dead in sins, hath quickened us together with Christ, (by grace ye are saved;) and hath raised us up together, and made us sit together in heavenly places in Christ Jesus: That in the ages to come he might shew the exceeding riches of his grace in his kindness toward us through Christ Jesus." The key to these verses is the phrase, "the ages to come." The presence of Jesus in your life must be evident right now in this life.

Colossians 1:27 says, "...Christ in you, the hope of glory." God's presence or will can only be demonstrated by His presence in your life. He is in you and wants your life to **define** the perfect will of God: spirit, soul and body.

Ephesians 3:20-21 says, "Now unto him that is able to do exceeding abundantly above all that we ask or think, according to the power that worketh in us, unto him be glory in the church by Christ

Jesus throughout all ages, world without end. Amen." You see here that God's will is **defined** through Jesus for the Church. God's will has not changed. His **definition** for life is still summed up in one word—JESUS!

God won't make you receive life or enjoy life, but He will see that you are made aware of its availability. Deuteronomy 30:19 says, "I call heaven and earth to record this day against you, that I have set before you life and death, blessing and cursing: therefore choose life, that both thou and thy seed may live." God spoke this in the Old Testament to the people of Israel. The choice is the same today and Jesus said He was that life. In John 10:10 Jesus says, "The thief cometh not, but for to steal, and to kill, and to destroy: I am come that they might have life, and that they might have it more abundantly." The choice is yours. The **definition** is the same—Jesus is the life and perfect will of God!

PRAY THIS//

Father, I know religion isn't relevant so I determine to live a life that expresses Your will and brings attention to You, in Jesus' name, Amen.

CONFESS THIS//

Jesus lives big in me and He will do exceeding, abundantly above all that I can ask or even think.

//Chapter Eight

GRACE & TRUTH

A major stumbling block for most Christians is the ability to maintain the right emphasis on Scripture. You don't have to be a degreed theologian in order to understand and enjoy the promises of God. However, you do have to believe God provided them through Jesus and that His grace will give you access to all you need through faith.

This "grace thing" is somewhat misunderstood, but it doesn't have to be. God simply made a covenant with Himself to allow mankind to have access to a supernatural re-connect through the blood of His Son, Jesus. Grace is God simply saying, "I'm doing this because I love you and am willing to adopt you into My family just because I WANT TO!" What a deal and it's all because God determined to provide Himself a Lamb on your behalf.

Without going into a lot of detail, I want to show you something from the book of Genesis that reflects Jesus as the **definition** and express image of God. Genesis 22:7-8 says, "And Isaac spake unto Abraham his father, and said, My father: and he said, Here am I, my son. And he said, Behold the fire and the wood: but where is the lamb for a burnt offering? And Abraham said, My son, GOD WILL PROVIDE HIMSELF A LAMB for a burnt offering: so they went both of them together" (emphasis mine). You talk about a couple of faith men! Remember, Abraham began in verse 5 of this chapter by telling the men who came with him, "I and the lad will go yonder and worship, and come again to you." Abraham knew that he was on a mission to offer his son, Isaac, as a sacrifice, as God had instructed. These words show that Abraham had so much faith and confidence in God and His Word that he knew God would do whatever it took, including raising Isaac from the dead if necessary, to keep His promises. Wow!

How about you? Will God do the same for you? Of course He will. You now have a better covenant based on better promises, SEALED WITH THE BLOOD OF JESUS. Hebrews 8:6 tells us, "But now hath he obtained a more excellent ministry, by how much also he is the mediator of a better covenant, which was established upon better promises." Hebrews 10:19 says, "Having therefore, brethren, boldness to enter into the holiest by the blood of Jesus." And 1 Peter 1:12 reminds us, "Unto whom it was revealed, that not unto themselves, but unto us they did minister the things, which are now reported unto you by them that have preached the gospel unto you with the Holy Ghost sent down from heaven; which things the angels desire to look into."

Generally, Christians live under such a works or sin consciousness that they are unable to accept the grace of God revealed through Jesus. Denominationalism has kept most people bound in religious tradition to the point of being spiritually incarcerated. Most people have been so deceived that they don't have any concept of God's true grace, mercy and truth when it comes to His love for them and the power to transform their lives.

How about you? Are you enjoying what Jesus paid for you to receive or are you just going through the motions? Has your Christianity provided answers or just more questions? Jesus came to reveal the perfect will of God, so don't settle for less.

John 1:14-18 clearly teaches us, "And the Word was made flesh, and dwelt among us, (and we beheld his glory, the glory as of the ONLY BEGOTTEN of the Father,) full of grace and truth. John bare witness of him, and cried, saying, This was he of whom I spake, He that cometh after me is preferred before me: for he was before me. And of his fullness have all we received, and grace for grace. For the law was given by Moses, but GRACE and TRUTH came by Jesus Christ. No man hath seen God at any time; the only begotten Son, which is in the bosom of the Father, he hath declared him" (emphasis mine). In these verses you clearly see that Jesus is the **definition** of God and through Him GRACE and TRUTH are revealed. It's time you see Jesus for who He really is, the express image of God in every way for all mankind.

It's time to stop settling for some mediocre sub-standard existence, when grace and truth are available to you. When Jesus said in John 10:10

that He came to give you life more abundantly, He wasn't talking about in the sweet by and by but in the nasty now. The grace, mercy, love, power and truth of God's Word is just as alive today as when Jesus walked the earth. In the name of Jesus, don't settle for maybe or I hope so, when all the promises in Christ Jesus are YES and AMEN! Get with the truth and the truth will set you free because that's what Jesus paid for...FREEDOM.

Pray This//

Father, thank You for Your grace and for making a way for me to re-connect with You through the precious blood of Jesus, in Jesus' name, Amen.

Confess This//

I choose to walk in the abundant life that Jesus paid for me to receive. I am free!

QUESTIONS/ ANSWERS

Q. I've always been taught that God is in control. If that's not the case, then who is?

A. This is not an easy question to answer quickly, but it is an easy question to answer! Because Adam and Eve disobeyed God's command concerning eating of the tree of the knowledge of good and evil, Satan was given control of this world's system. You see this in 2 Corinthians 4:4, "In whom the god of this world (Satan) hath blinded the minds of them which believe not, lest the light of the glorious gospel of Christ, who is the image of God, should shine unto them."

Adam and Eve had originally been given authority over the earth, as you read from Genesis 1:26, "And God said, Let us make man in our image (spirit), after our likeness: and let them have dominion over the fish of the sea, and over the fowl of the air, and over the cattle, and over all the earth, and over every creeping thing that creepeth on the earth" (explanation mine). Obviously "control" was originally given to man, but as man sometimes does, he blew it. So how can you continue to say, "God is in control"? Because by His death and resurrection, Jesus restored dominion to you. Jesus says to us in Luke 10:19, "Behold, I give unto you power to tread on serpents (deception) and scorpions (distractions), and over all the power of the enemy: and nothing shall by any means hurt you" (explanation mine).

You have been given a free will and the power to choose. The Holy Spirit spoke it to my heart this way years ago: "My sovereignty is best expressed in My unwillingness to use My power to force Myself on anyone." If God won't MAKE people choose His Son and go to Heaven in spite of His great love and desire for none to perish, why would He endeavor to control anything else that will all pass away anyway? Matthew 24:35 reminds us, "Heaven and earth shall pass away, but my words shall not pass away."

Q. Okay, but doesn't God judge people and cause bad things to happen to get their attention? You know, like 9/11, Katrina, earthquakes, wars, and stuff like that?

A. NO, NO, NO, NO, NO. The thief, Satan, is in the earth with the primary goal of stealing, killing and destroying. If a situation arises having anything to do with these things, it is him, NOT GOD! John 10:10 says, "The thief cometh not, but for to steal, and to kill, and to destroy: I am come that they might have life, and that they might have it more abundantly."

It is obvious according to the Word that God loves, forgives and provides eternal life to those who believe on Jesus. John 3:16-17 says, "For God so loved the world, that he gave his only begotten Son, that whosoever believeth in him should not perish, but have everlasting life. For God sent not his Son into the world to condemn the world; but that the world through him might be saved." This makes it crystal clear that Jesus' mission was to save, not to condemn or judge. Lastly, 2 Timothy 4:1 says, "I charge thee therefore before God, and the Lord Jesus Christ, who shall judge the quick and the dead AT HIS APPEARING and HIS KINGDOM" (emphasis mine). The judgment of God is reserved for Jesus' return and that will not be a natural disaster, but a supernatural event.

Q. If Satan is the god of this world, then how can I be successful against him?

A. Jesus' primary goal was to restore the authority Adam and Eve had been given in the earth. First John 3:8 says, "He that committeth sin is of the devil; for the devil sinneth from the beginning. For this purpose the Son of God was manifested, that he might destroy the works of the devil." Then Colossians 2:13-15 says, "And you, being dead in your sins and the uncircumcision of your flesh, hath he quickened together with him, having forgiven you all trespasses; blotting out the handwriting of ordinances that was against us, which was contrary to us, and took it out of the way, nailing it to his cross; and having spoiled principalities and powers, he made a shew of them openly, triumphing over them in it."

Revelation 1:18 makes it abundantly clear that Jesus has regained the authority for you and then gave it to you as stated in Luke 10:19. Revelation 1:18 says, "I am he that liveth, and was dead; and, behold, I am alive for evermore, Amen; and have the keys of hell and death." Jesus tells us in Luke 10:19, "Behold, I give unto you power to tread on serpents (deception) and scorpions (distractions), and over all the power of the enemy: and nothing shall by any means hurt you" (explanation mine). Everything Jesus paid for, including the defeat of Satan, is now yours by faith in and through Him! The devil is a defeated foe and every believer can enforce his defeat.

Q. How do I exercise my authority over the devil?

A. You exercise your authority the same way Jesus did, by knowing what the Word says and then reminding the devil that IT IS WRITTEN! Notice the example Jesus gives us in Matthew 4:4,7,10 says, "But he answered and said, It is written, Man shall not live by bread alone, but by every word that proceedeth out of the mouth of God... Jesus said unto him, It is written again, Thou shalt not tempt the Lord thy God...Then saith Jesus unto him, Get thee hence, Satan: for it is written, Thou shalt worship the Lord thy God, and him only shalt thou serve."

In Acts 3:6 we see this account, "Then Peter said, Silver and gold have I none; but such as I have give I thee: In the name of JESUS CHRIST OF NAZARETH rise up and walk" (emphasis mine). Have you ever wondered why as time goes on, it's the NAME of JESUS that comes under such heat in almost every arena of life, from churches to government? The fact that the NAME of JESUS has been removed from prayers as well as government settings is proof that it is that NAME of JESUS that makes the difference! Philippians 2:9-10 says, "Wherefore God also hath highly exalted him, and given him a name which is above every name: That at the name of JESUS every knee should bow, of things in heaven, and things in earth, and things under the earth; And that every tongue should confess that JESUS is LORD, to the glory of GOD the FATHER" (emphasis mine). Authority and power begins and ends with the Word of God and the NAME of JESUS. Use them in faith and you will have the victory.

Q. Why do good Christian people have as many problems as those in the world?

A. It's up to you to find out for yourself the authority and power you've been given in and through the Word and the name of Jesus. Just because a person is a Christian doesn't make them immune from the attacks of the enemy. Hosea 4:6 says, "My people are destroyed for a lack of knowledge." James 1:25 makes your responsibility so clear, "But whoso looketh into the perfect law of liberty, and continueth therein, he being not a forgetful hearer, but a doer of the work, this man shall be blessed in his deed." Just hearing the Word is not enough. You must do it in order to be blessed.

Every promise has a condition, so in order to walk in and experience them, you must work out the SALVATION you've been given. Philippians 2:12 says, "Wherefore, my beloved, as ye have always obeyed, not only in my presence only, but now much more in my absence, work out your own salvation with fear (respect) and trembling (awe)" (explanation mine). This verse makes it clear that you have a part to play in your walk of faith and victory. Jesus paid for victory but you must believe and do your part.

Q. If God wants people healed and prosperous, why doesn't He just make it happen?

A. People are not puppets that God can do with as He pleases. You must make a determination to obey and use the tools He's given you. Because you were created in God's image (according to Genesis 1:26), you are a free moral agent and you can will to do or will not to do whatever you want. Deuteronomy 30:19 speaks the same today as it did to the people of Israel, "I call heaven and earth to record (or witness) this day against you, that I have set before you life and death, blessing and cursing: therefore choose life, that both thou and thy seed may live" (explanation mine). You must be willing to do your part. When you find a promise in the Word of God concerning healing, prosperity or whatever, it's up to you to first of all simply believe and then do what's necessary to experience the promise.

Acts 10:38 is one of my favorite verses concerning healing and deliverance being the perfect will of God for all mankind. It says, "How God anointed Jesus of Nazareth with the Holy Ghost and with power: who went about doing good, and healing all that were oppressed of the devil; for God was with him." Knowing the will of God should cause you to WANT THE WILL OF GOD FOR YOUR LIFE!

One final verse sums up your responsibility when it comes to receiving prosperity and health for your life. Third John 2 says, "Beloved, I wish (or pray) above all things that thou mayest prosper and be in health, even as thy soul prospereth" (explanation mine). Your soul is made up of your mind, will and emotions and they must become servants to the Word of God before the Word of God will serve you. Renew your mind, and the promises will happen.

Q. Are all bad things the result of sin or disobedience in the life of a believer?

A. You have a part to play in the affairs of your life. Seedtime and harvest, sowing and reaping, these are principles that will affect everything you do and consequently must be considered. Genesis 8:22 says, "While the earth remaineth, seedtime and harvest, and cold and heat, and summer and winter, and day and night shall not cease." Galatians 6:7 also says, "Be not deceived; God is not mocked: for whatsoever a man soweth, that shall he also reap." According to Romans 6:23, "the wages of sin is death." The problem is obviously not just the devil. He is going to do everything he can to make your life miserable but it's up to you to recognize his tactics and then make changes for yourself. One of the best ways to avoid problems is to hook up with people who are experiencing the promises of God and are reaching out to others. You cannot do this alone, God wants you to be a part of the body of Christ.

Q. Is Jesus really the only way to Heaven?

A. This is one of my favorite questions, especially considering the day in which we live. So many

Christians, including ministers, are so concerned about being *politically correct* that they won't take a Word of God stand in regard to this question. The only thing I'm going to live by is what God's Word says because it is the only revelation of His will. Jesus said Himself in John 14:6, "I am the way, the truth, and the life: no man cometh unto the Father, but by me." Now I'm going to be honest with you, if that's the only reference I had, it would be more than enough. If JESUS said He was THE ONLY WAY, I'm going to believe there is no other way!

Peter also made it clear that through no other name could one be saved when he said in Acts 4:10-12, "Be it known unto you all, and to all the people of Israel, that by the name of Jesus Christ of Nazareth, whom ye crucified, whom God raised from the dead, even by him doth this man stand here before you whole. This is the stone which was set at nought of you builders, which is become the head of the corner. Neither is there SALVATION IN ANY OTHER: for there is NONE OTHER NAME under heaven given among men, whereby we must be SAVED" (emphasis mine).

Last but not least, God mentioned no alternatives in John 3:16. As a Holy Bible believer, you can lift the name of Jesus and then He can do the saving as it says in John 12:32, "And I, if I be lifted up from the earth, will draw all men unto me." Jesus was lifted up in the crucifixion. Now, if He's lifted up as the only Messiah, He can save those who believe.

CONCLUSION

For those who don't know Jesus as Lord, would you like to know Him?

If you were to die today, where would you spend eternity? If you have accepted Jesus Christ as your Lord and Savior, you can be assured that when you die, you will go directly into the presence of God in Heaven. If you haven't made this decision, is there any reason why you can't make it right now? God will accept you just as you are if you will accept His Son right now! Pray this prayer out loud in sincerity and faith, and you will be born again.

PRAY THIS//

Father, I come to You in the name of Jesus to receive salvation and eternal life. I believe that Jesus is Your Son. I believe He died on the cross for my sins and that You raised Him from the dead. I receive Jesus now and make Him the Lord of my life. Jesus, come into my life. I welcome You as my Lord and Savior. Father, I believe Your Word. I confess with my mouth and believe in my heart that I am saved and born again. I am now a child of God, in Jesus' name, Amen.

FOR THOSE WHO ARE NOT FILLED WITH THE HOLY SPIRIT, WOULD YOU LIKE TO BE FILLED?

There's more to Christianity than just being born again and having your ticket to Heaven. The Holy Spirit is God's voice in the earth today. God speaks to you by the Spirit and being filled with the Holy Spirit is received by faith. Acts 1:8 says, "But ye shall receive power, after that the Holy Ghost is come upon you." "Power for what?" you might ask. It is the power and authority He desires you, as His child, walk in every day. You were designed to have dominion, not walk around in defeat. (Genesis 1:26 and John 16:33.)

The evidence of being filled with the Holy Spirit is speaking in tongues. Acts 2:4 says, "And they were all filled with the Holy Ghost, and began to speak with other tongues, as the Spirit gave them utterance." When you speak in tongues you are "building yourself up on your most holy faith," basically charging your spiritual battery for service in God's Kingdom. When you are praying in tongues, you are praying the will of God. Romans 8:26-27 says, "Likewise the Spirit also helpeth our infirmities: for we know not what we should pray for as we ought: but the Spirit Himself maketh intercession for us with groanings which cannot be uttered. And he that searcheth the hearts knoweth what is the mind of the Spirit, because he maketh intercession for the saints according to the will of God."

PRAY THIS//

Father, I am Your child and I believe Your Word which says that if I will just ask, I will receive the infilling of the Holy Spirit with the evidence of speaking in other tongues. (Luke 11:13.) I want this power in my life to be an effective witness (Acts 1:8), so I open my mouth and begin to speak in other tongues as the Holy Spirit gives me utterance, in Jesus' name, Amen.

Now, begin to speak what you hear in your spirit (heart) because you have received the power of the Holy Spirit.

ABOUT THE AUTHOR

Pastor Dean Shropshire left secular employment over 22 years ago to pursue the call of God on his life. Together with his wife Kathy, he pioneered chooselife CHURCH in Hobbs, New Mexico. They held the first service on Easter in 1989.

Pastor Dean preaches a message of hope, restoration, and change that stems from knowing the character of God and its revelation manifested through the life of Jesus.

As an extension of Dean Shropshire Ministries, Pastor Dean and the staff of chooselife CHURCH inaugurated DEEP Bible Training Center in 2006.

Dean's desire is for believers to understand that God is for them, that the Word of God works, and that they can live out the abundant life that Jesus paid for them to have. His wife of over 33 years, Kathy, and his two daughters, Charity and Faith, and son-in-law, Greg, join Dean in ministry.

In his spare time, Dean enjoys reading, shopping with his family, and cheering for the Yankees.

Dean Shropshire Ministries is committed to sharing the reality that there is always more available for the lives of those who would choose life!

John 10:10/Deuteronomy 30:19

AUTHOR CONTACT INFORMATION

If you would like more information about this book or other materials by Pastor Dean Shropshire, please use the information below to contact us. We would love to hear from you!

Dean Shropshire Ministries
P.O. Box 22
Hobbs, New Mexico 88240
Phone: 575.397.4604

www.chooselifehobbs.com